FOOLED YOU!

DEBASHISH MAJUMDAR

ILLUSTRATED BY
NILOUFER WADIA

SCHOLASTIC
New York Toronto London Auckland
Sydney New Delhi Hong Kong

To my parents from childhood – grandparents (Dadu and Didima)
~ Debashish Majumdar

For my little girl, who also thinks she knows everything.
~ Niloufer Wadia

Published by Scholastic India Pvt. Ltd.
A subsidiary of Scholastic Inc., New York, 10012 (USA).
Publishers since 1920, with international operations in Canada, Australia, New Zealand, the United Kingdom, India, and Hong Kong.

For information regarding permission, write to:
Scholastic India Pvt. Ltd.
A-27, Ground Floor, Sigma Centre
Infocity-1, Sector 34, Gurgaon 122001 (India)

This reprint edition: January 2024

ISBN-13: 978-93-5275-301-7

Printed at Sanat Printers, Kundli, Haryana.

‘April Fool? Not me!’
Rina grins.

‘There’s cherry custard in the fridge,’ Ma smiles.

'April Fool? Not me!'
Rina giggles.

‘There’s a new mobile phone in my car.
Go, take it!’ Dad calls out.

'April Fool? Not me!' Rina titters.

'I have the latest mystery novel in my school bag,' says Rohan dada.

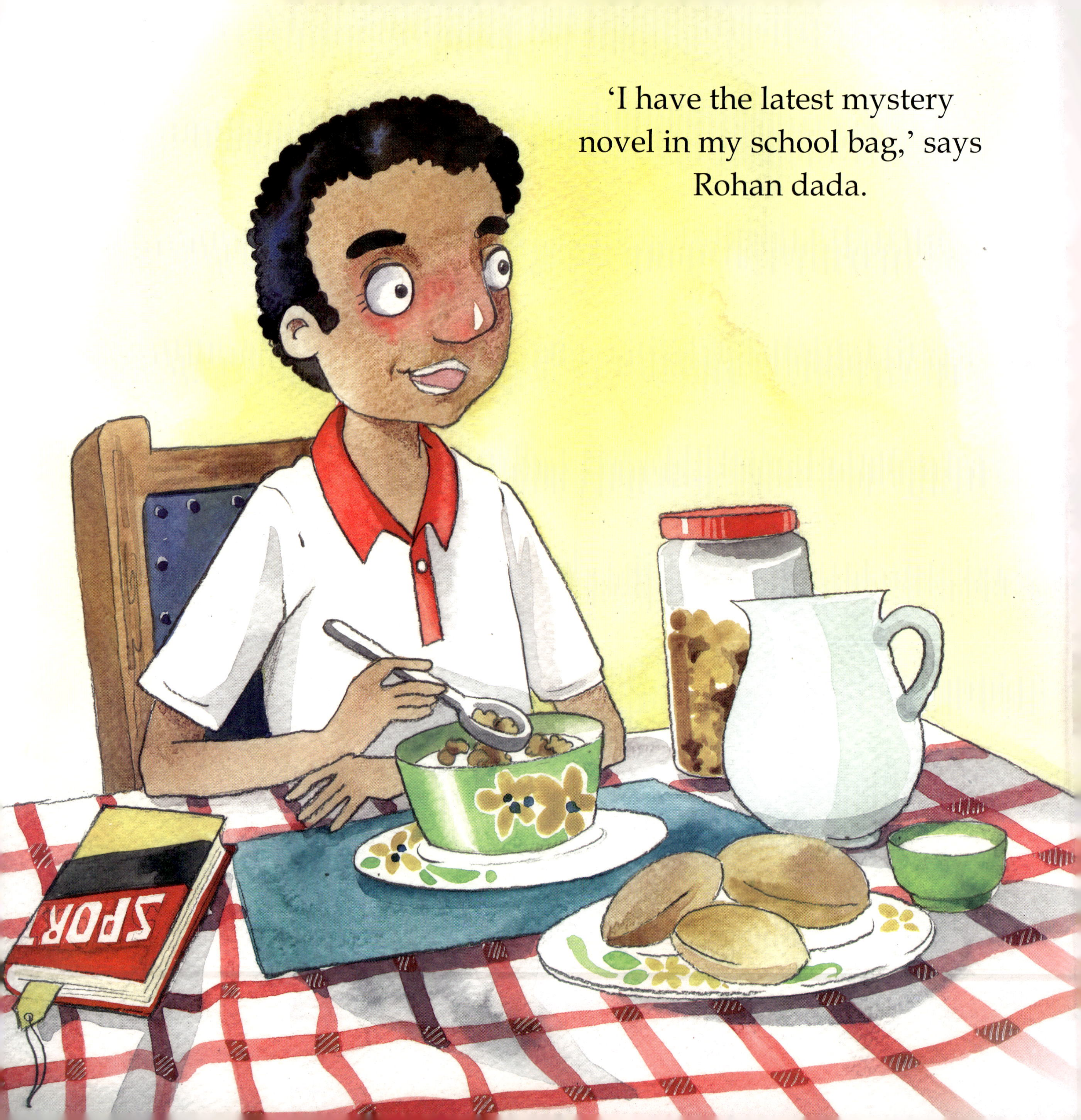

'April Fool?
Not me!'
Rina laughs.

At school, her friend Anita exclaims, 'Wow, Rina! You've won the medal for the best all-rounder in the class.'

'April Fool? Not me!' Rina gleams.

Back home Rina finds …

Dad is reading the mystery novel.

… Rohan dada is slurping her favourite cherry custard.

… and Ma is talking to her best friend over a new mobile phone.

‘Rina has won the medal for best all-rounder in class. I saw it on the school notice board,’ she beams.

'Oh no!' burst out Rina. 'So, it's all true! I thought today was April Fool's Day!'

'Oh yes,' Ma, Dad and Rohan dada laughed together. 'We all forgot today was April Fool's Day, Rina!'

'How silly of me,'
mumbled Rina.

The doorbell rang. Ma opened the door to see it was Grandma.

Putting a box on the table, she called out, 'Rina, look at the beautiful puppy I've got for you!'

Rina ran to
Grandma eagerly.

‘April Fool, Rina!’
Grandma winked and
hugged her.

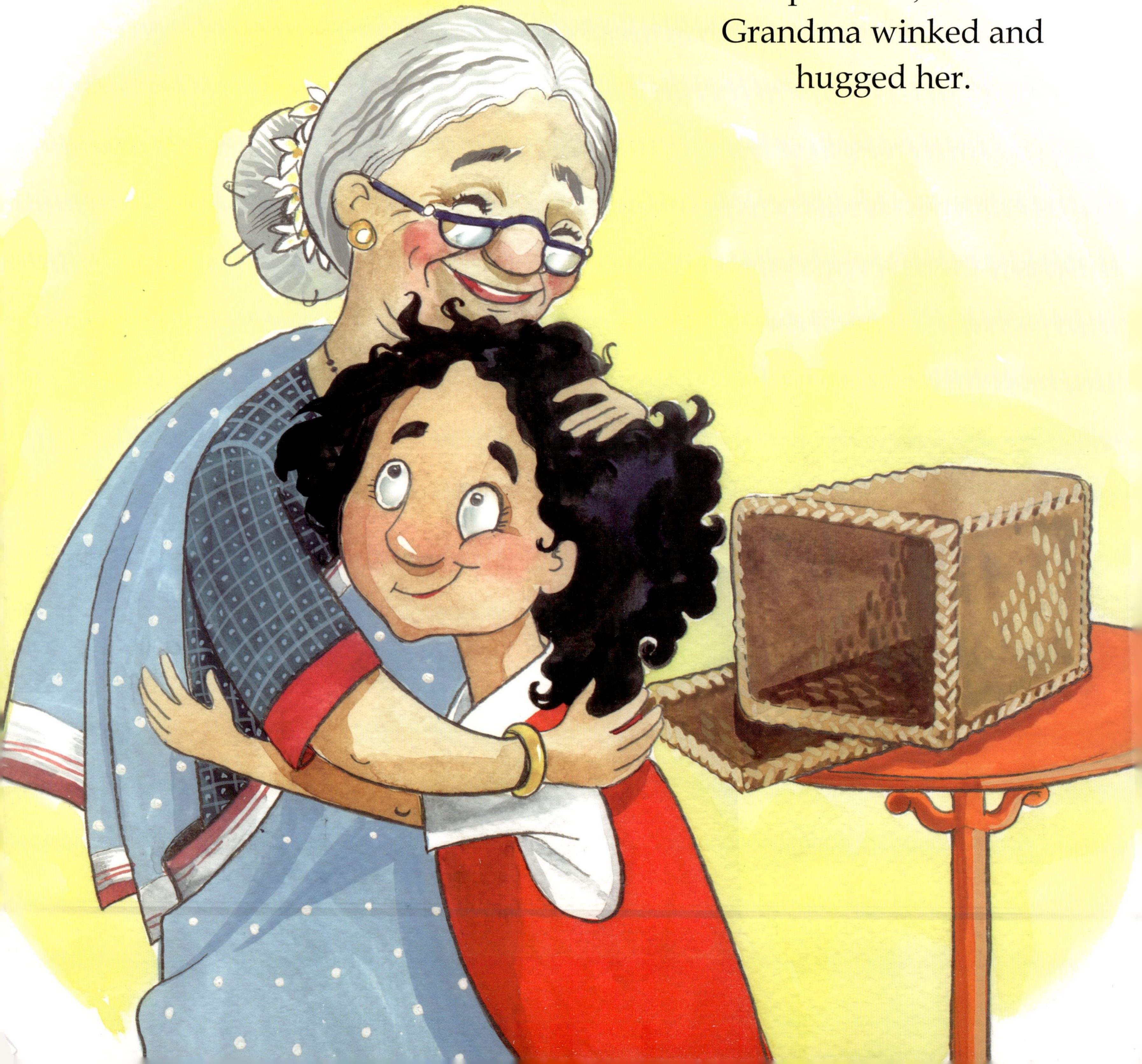

About the Author

Debashish Majumdar is a qualified marketing professional from The Chartered Institute of Marketing, UK and has spent over 20 years as a copywriter and advertising consultant. He has won a dozen national writing awards for children and was Shortlisted for a Commonwealth Short Story Award in 2003. His works appear in 17 books in addition to the *Chicken Soup for the Soul* series. Debashish has also written over 250 stories for children, which have appeared in mostly all national newspapers/magazines.

About the Illustrator

Niloufer Wadia spent over 20 years in advertising before deciding to leave suddenly to follow her first love—illustration and painting—and find out if she could make a career of it. It turns out, she could. She now has almost a dozen children's picture books to her name and hopes to continue doing them. She lives in Pune with her daughter.

OTHER PICTURE BOOKS

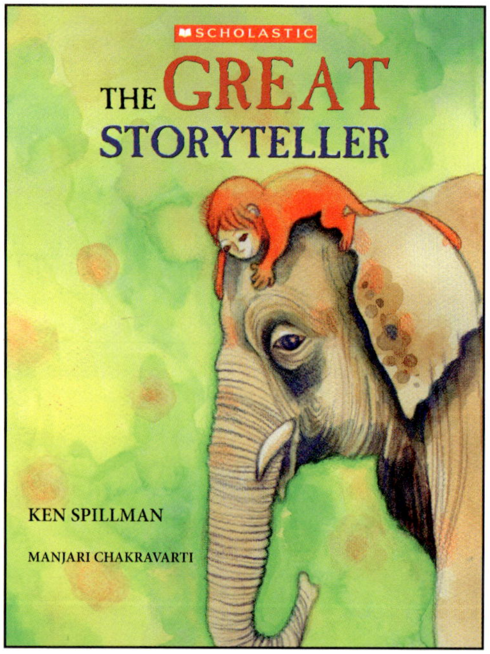